BOOKS IN THIS SERIES

1. Super Dweeb and the Pencil of Destiny
2. Super Dweeb Vs Doctor Eraser-Butt
3. Super Dweeb Vs the Evil Doodler
4. Super Dweeb and the Time Trumpet
5. Super Dweeb Vs Count Dorkula
6. Super Dweeb and the Snack Attack

This edition published in 2025 by Arcturus Publishing Limited, 26/27 Bickels Yard, 151-153 Bermondsey Street, London SE1 3HA

Copyright © Arcturus Holdings Limited

All rights reserved. No part of this publication may be reproduced, stored in a retrieval system, or transmitted, in any form or by any means, electronic, mechanical, photocopying, recording, or otherwise, without prior written permission in accordance with the provisions of the Copyright Act 1956 (as amended). Any person or persons who do any unauthorized act in relation to this publication may be liable to criminal prosecution and civil claims for damages.

Words and pictures: Jess Bradley
Design: Stefan Holliland and Nathan Balsom
Original concept: Joe Harris
Art direction: Rosie Bellwood-Moyler

ISBN: 978-1-3988-5054-5

CH012694NT
Supplier 13, Date 0425, PI 00009296

Printed in China

CONTENTS

Part 1: SUPER DWEEB and the Pencil of Destiny

Chapter 1	The Trouble with Mr. Squibb	10
Chapter 2	The World's Worst Field Trip	18
Chapter 3	Escape from Fallout Island	30
Chapter 4	Pencil Power!	38
Chapter 5	The Scribble Monster	48
Chapter 6	The Awesome Battle	61

Part 2: SUPER DWEEB Vs Doctor Eraser-Butt

Chapter 7	Dweeb Life	74
Chapter 8	Sinister Super Spy Squad	80
Chapter 9	Super Dweeb Fan Club	88
Chapter 10	Doctor Eraser-Butt's Secret Origin	96
Chapter 11	No Ifs, One Butt	102
Chapter 12	Kid Crayon Investigates	110
Chapter 13	Team-Up Time	123
Chapter 14	Back at Dweeb HQ	130

Part 3: SUPER DWEEB Vs the Evil Doodler

Chapter 15	Keeping Up with the Dweebs	136
Chapter 16	Too Many Andys	144
Chapter 17	Bad Times!	162
Chapter 18	The Temple of Gloom	170
Chapter 19	Andy Vs Anti-Andy	180

HOW TO DRAW SUPER DWEEB AND FRIENDS 197

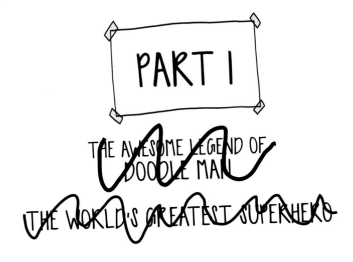

SUPER DWEEB
AND THE PENCIL OF DESTINY

WHO'S WHO?

ANDY! Schoolkid and secret superhero

Awesome rating: THE AWESOMEST

MONA! Andy's best friend and tech genius

Awesome rating: ELEVEN OUT OF TEN

OSCAR! Andy's annoying little brother

Awesome rating: NOT VERY

MEAN MIKE! A school bully

Awesome rating: THE EXACT OPPOSITE OF AWESOME

THE PENCIL OF DESTINY!

A radioactive pencil that can bring doodles to life!

Awesome rating: OFF THE SCALE

Hi, I'm ANDY. Nice to meet you, person reading this! I'll call you P.R.T. for short. (You're cool with that, right, P.R.T.?) I'm a pretty normal kid. A bit dweeby, maybe. I can't catch a **football** or dance but I can draw pretty much <u>ANYTHING.</u> Except for hands, which are really hard.

This is the incredible TRUE STORY of how I became a SUPERHERO. (Yes, really!)

Chapter 1   The Trouble with Mr. Squibb

"Andy! ANDY! ANNNDDDYYY! Are you paying attention in class or are you DRAWING AGAIN?"

Uh-oh. This sounded like a problem that not even ACE SILVERBACK, maverick space-gorilla cop, could solve. I had been completely lost in thought, happily doodling the latest cosmic adventure in my awesome SPACE APE™ series.

But I wasn't being threatened by evil alien octopods in the ghastly Gamma Quadrant. No, the truth was much worse—I was in Mr. Squibb's MATH CLASS. And Mr. Squibb did NOT look happy.

"The last time I checked, we were not studying ART. We were studying algebra. And these ... monkeys and squid ... are definitely NOT ALGEBRA!"

"Um, it's an ape and an octopus actually," I mumbled. "Not a squibb—I mean, a squid." Several of the class sniggered.

"I don't CARE!" said Mr. Squibb, "Drawing pictures won't get you anywhere in life."

Mr. Squibb is <u>SUPER-BORING</u>. If I had to write reports for my teachers, this is what I would send home to his parents.

MR. SQUIBB'S REPORT CARD

Your son, Mr. Squibb, has no imagination. Like, literally, zero. His favorite book is the dishwasher manual. He can suck the fun and excitement out of absolutely anything—like some kind of super-powerful fun vacuum cleaner. (Except that sounds sort of cool, so forget that.) Grade: ZZZ (for snoring).

"Are you paying attention, ANDY?" Somehow, Mr. Squibb was still speaking. "As I was saying—that's why today we will be taking a field trip. A highly educational field trip. Everyone take a leaflet and pass it on."

I took one of the leaflets and read it.

"We also have a new student! This is MONA. Why don't you tell us a little bit about yourself?"

SO COOL!

"We moved here from Battsburg so my dad could study AI at the university. This town smells funny. <u>NOT GOOD FUNNY</u>."

"Um, super! Well, why don't you go and take a seat with Andy? In fact, you can be his BUDDY on the school trip!"

Of course everyone laughed. A COOL person being buddies with ME?

Tie (I like ties! They're fancy!)

Most likely to join every school club.

Thick glasses (I like them).

Full of super interesting facts.

Good at drawing (but not hands).

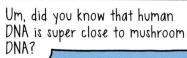

Ugh, it's Mean Mike! Every class has that one kid destined to be a super villain and Mike is in MINE! We've been in the same class since first grade and he lives to make my life a MISERY! (I think he's just jealous of my drawing skills.)

Mike is always surrounded by his goons:

ME AND MEAN MIKE: A BRIEF HISTORY

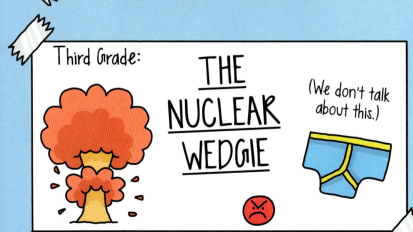

Chapter 2 The World's Worst Field Trip

Soon... "Okay everyone, on the bus!" said Mr. Squibb.

I couldn't wait to get to Fallout Island and do some sketching.

Maybe I'd get some cool ideas for my Space Ape comic!

"Now, Mike, you've already got three detentions this week

and it's only 10a.m. on Monday!" said Mr. Squibb.

"You have your whole life to be a jerk! Why don't you just take a day off and give us a break?"

Wow, that's the first time that anyone has ever talked to Mike that way.

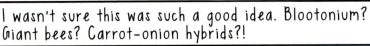

And we were on **FALLOUT ISLAND!**

"Watch your step, children! Yar!" said Captain Poopdeck.

"Captain, why does your EYEPATCH keep switching eyes?" I asked.

"I have no idea what ye be talking about! Yar!" said Captain Poopdeck.

Mr. Squibb rounded us all up and we headed off. For a radiation-filled **HAZARD**, it was actually pretty scenic!

"Okay class, time for a hike! Pay particular attention to the **MUTATED** flora!"

If Squirrelzilla hadn't been chasing us, I would have stopped to

SKETCH him! We ran through the woods back to the dock.

"Quick, through here! Maybe we can lose him!" I shouted.

Luckily, it looked like Squirrelzillas weren't too **INTELLIGENT!**

I ran to grab my pencil.

"Wow, look at this!" I said.

"Never mind that thing! Run before that radiated rodent **WAKES UP!!**" shouted Mona.

29

Chapter 3   Escape from Fallout Island

But when we reached the dock...

"*NOOOO!*" I shrieked.

"They left without us! I don't believe this! Trapped on a radioactive island with a mutant squirrel! GASP! Maybe we'll mutate too!"

Mona sighed. "Oh, CALM DOWN! We just need to think logically about this. Here's your stupid giant pencil!"

"I don't want to live here and eat those weird carrot-onions forever!" I said.

"Stop being so DRAMATIC! It's a shame you can't draw yourself out of this!"

"Hmm, maybe I CAN!"

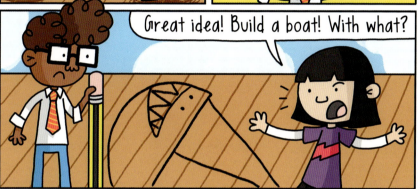

The boat I had drawn <u>C A M E T O L I F E</u>!

Mona poked it. "It's real!" she said. "Wow, I take back all of my sarcasm! The blootonium must have done something to your pencil!"

Just then, the monster reappeared.

"Oh no, Squirrelzilla woke up and now he looks even ANGRIER! We have to go!" I said.

"I think he wants your pencil," said Mona.

"Nothing at all! *EVERYONE* should be a dweeb!" I replied.

Mona quickly changed the subject. "We should talk about this pencil and this boat. Will it get us back to the mainland?"

"I guess we'll find out," I said.

During dinner, all I could think about was testing out my new pencil!

I wolfed down everything and headed to my room. "Finished! I'm off to do my HOMEWORK!"

"Dishes first," said Mom. Argh! "But my homework!" I whined.

Stuff I drew with the pencil that came to life!

A sausage with legs

A friendly robot

Squishy octopus

A T. rex (I made sure he was very small!)

A hand (TERRIFYING!!)

SPLAT-CHAT V 2.0

 ARTY GUY: So I drew a bunch of things with the pencil in my sketchbook and they all came to life!!

 COOL GRRL: The radiation must have altered the molecular structure of the atoms in the pencil!

 ARTY GUY: Uh... yeah... just what I was thinking! 😂

 COOL GRRL: 😋 Sure it was! How long did each doodle last before it disappeared?

 ARTY GUY: Around 10 mins, which is good because I drew a hand and it was the scariest thing ever!!

 COOL GRRL: Ha ha! Better watch what you draw! Hmm, maybe the bigger the sketch, the longer it lasts?

 ARTY GUY: Makes sense! I have to go. See you @ school tomorrow!

 COOL GRRL: Bring the pencil!! Also, your Gamma Guys fic was pretty cool!

Chapter 4   Pencil Power!

Of course, living with a little brother is a risk to magic pencil security...

"What have you got?" Oscar asked.

"NOTHING! It's a ... project for school!" I said hastily.

I knew I'd get some funny looks at the bus stop but I didn't care—
I had a magic pencil!

I messaged Mona when I got on the bus...

"Ugh, I'm not ready for a POP QUIZ!" I groaned.

"Well, we do have a solution to that," Mona said with a grin.

"Set off the fire alarm?" I asked.

Mona rolled her eyes. "The PENCIL!"

FUN WE HAD WITH THE PENCIL!

Drawing a gang of raccoons to chase Mean Mike and his goons!

RACCOONS!

ENTERTAINING THE SCHOOL WITH A GIANT DANCING PINEAPPLE!

FIREWORK DISPLAY!

THIS PENCIL IS...

...100% AWESOME

SHAKE SHAKE SHAKE!

What's going on?!

Everything disappears after 10 minutes! POP!

43

Mr. Squibb and the principle were going crazy by the end of the day...

"And then an ELEPHANT chased me through the cafeteria!"

"I didn't like that DANCING PINEAPPLE one bit!"

Everyone was talking about it! I felt like I had the best secret in the world. Mona wasn't as enthusiastic about it though...

"Okay, today has been fun and all but we really can't do anything like this again," she said.

"Oh, you worry too much! What could POSSIBLY go wrong with a MAGIC PENCIL that makes art come to life?"

"This is so much fun! I love this pencil!"

Things were looking so **SWEET** right now! Anything was possible with this pencil. Maybe I could run for student president!

Chapter 5   The Scribble Monster

I woke up feeling great! I couldn't wait to do some more doodling!

BUT WAIT.

Um, **WHERE'S MY PENCIL?**

GONE!

I'm sure the pencil was right here!

Okay, don't panic! It must just be under my bed or in my closet...

But the pencil was **GONE!**

"Mona's going to be so totally unimpressed with me! I'll be hearing "I TOLD YOU SO" until the end of time!"

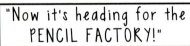

"ANDY, BREAKFAST!" Mom called.

I quickly got dressed and grabbed the pencil. Running down the stairs, I pointed at Oscar.

"YOU!" I hissed.

Mom came out of the kitchen.

"Everything okay, boys?" she asked.

"Heh heh, yeah! I'm just going to take Oscar to the park because I'm such a GOOD BROTHER!"

We raced out of the house and I told Oscar how much TROUBLE he had caused.

"This is terrible! I'm the one who's going to be grounded until I'm an old man! Never mind the hole in the side of our house!"

We RAN down the street and as we rounded a corner we ran into...

Mean Mike and his gang! Ugh, this was all I needed!

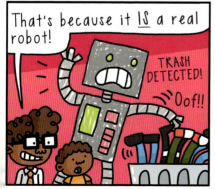

    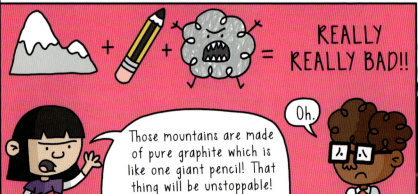

"NOW," said Mona, all business again, "I took the liberty of designing you a costume. Nobody can know you have a magic pencil. Or, you know, realize that we're the cause of all this trouble."

"Gasp! Like a **REAL SUPERHERO!**"

"Here, SUPER DWEEB! Go and get changed!" said Mona.

"Super Dweeb?" I grumbled. "Can't I have a cooler name?"

"Nope. I made the **COSTUME**, so I get to choose the name!"

"Hmph. Fair enough!"

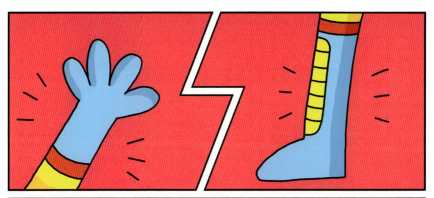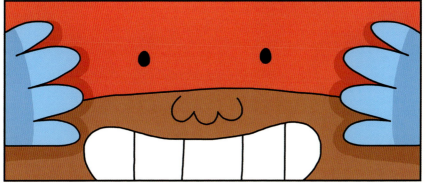

"Okay, no more heroic posing," said Mona. "We need to stop that monster!"

"But... how? It's <u>HUGE!</u>" I said.

Mona handed me an earpiece. "Here, put this in your ear. I'll be right here to guide you and try to figure out how we can defeat that thing!"

We can do this!

YEAH!

Andy, I'm sorry I unleashed a terrifying giant monster!

It's okay, Oscar. Do you think you could stay here and help Mona?

OKAY!

Chapter 6 The Awesome Battle

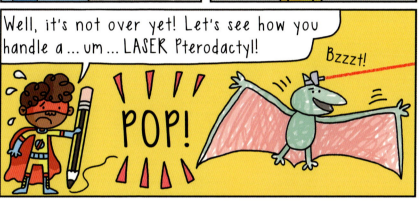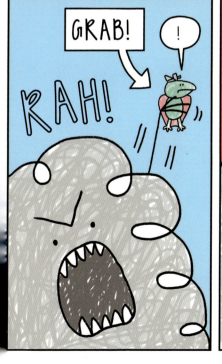

Back at Dweeb HQ...

"Okay," said Mona, "now let's have a chat about RESPONSIBILITY!"

"Heh heh!" I laughed. "Believe me, I think we've both learned our lesson!"

"Fine," sighed Mona. "Well, HOPEFULLY we won't have any more pencil-based excitement for a while. And if anyone asks where we've been today, just give them a MYSTERIOUS LOOK.

"You know, I <u>MIGHT</u> need some help from time to time, not just with the pencil. You saved the day with your canyon idea," I said.

"Just don't let it go to your head, okay?"

Chapter 7   Dweeb Life

Hey there, I'm ANDY. Here's a picture of me looking like I just had A REALLY GREAT IDEA! Everyone says that I'm a massive DWEEB—but my best friend MONA says that being a dweeb is <u>AWESOME</u>, and that I "totally own it."

Here are some things you should know about me!

—I like making my own COMIC BOOKS.

—Yes, I wear a tie. Yes, it's <u>on purpose.</u>

—I have a near-complete set of GAMMA GUYS trading cards. I'm just missing Roid-zilla™. Let me know if you have a spare!

Oh, and I'm a SECRET SUPERHERO.

Maybe I should have led with that.

This is me in my <u>costume.</u>

Ever since I became a superhero, I've had a lot on my plate.

MY "TO-DO" LIST:

FIGHT BAD GUYS!

DRAW AWESOME COMICS!

Don't forget homework!

LOOK AFTER OSCAR (MY LITTLE BROTHER)!

DO CHORES!

DEAL WITH FANS!

Hang out with my best friend!

 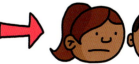
Make sure Mom and Dad don't find out about the whole SUPERHERO thing!

It's hard to juggle so much important stuff. Fortunately, I've come up with a sneaky solution! Before I go out crime fighting, I doodle a picture of <u>myself.</u>

Thanks to my ATOMIC PENCIL, anything that I draw comes to life!

Normally my living doodles only last ten minutes, but my "Andy-matter decoys" can live longer by eating normal pencils.

They can even do my homework for me!

 Of course, I feel pretty lousy about lying to my parents but it's all for the greater good, right? So far, I'm doing okay keeping everything in line. Now the only thing I **REALLY** need to do is get home before my parents read my ...

... report card. GULP!

Then Mom said the words that every superhero dreads:

"If you don't pass the big test tomorrow, you'll be GROUNDED!"

"Nooo!" I cried. "But I can't be grounded! I need to, uh…"

I sighed. "I guess I'll go study." I went upstairs to my room.

Chapter 8 Sinister Super Spy Squad

MEANWHILE, AT A TOP-SECRET BASE:

Where's my important Super Dweeb report, Dr. Sidebottom? I told you I needed it STAT!

Sorry, I was on my way to the staff canteen. They have tacos...

Wait a second, who are these guys? They weren't on the "Who's Who" page!

AGENT REGINA STORM

Top agent at A.C.R.O.N.Y.M., Regina doesn't stop until she gets the job done! No one messes with Regina Storm!

SKILLS: Unbelievable aim, super smart, mega sneaky, grand master at chess.

Height: Tall
Eyes: Scary
Hair: Perfect
Level: 10

Yikes! She seems very scary!

Hmm, he doesn't seem too scary...

DR. ERNEST SIDEBOTTOM

A brilliant scientist who enjoys tacos and likes reading and science experiments. Not entirely sure why he's working for A.C.R.O.N.Y.M.

SKILLS: Science stuff, cooking, pachisi, collecting decorative eggs.

Height: Short
Eyes: Nervous
Hair: Little to none
Level: 4

OPERATION DOODLE-BUG

SPIES' EYES ONLY

1. Acquire sample of pencil.

2. Make more pencils.

3. Build an army of cybernetic pencil cops to keep the world in check. <u>No more crime!</u>

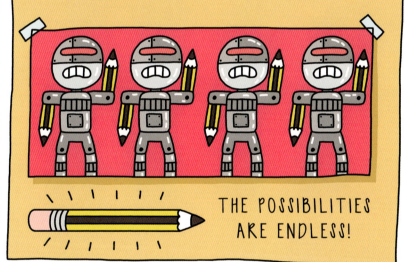

THE POSSIBILITIES ARE ENDLESS!

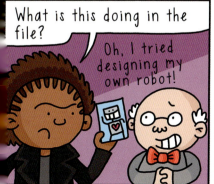

What is this doing in the file?

Oh, I tried designing my own robot!

Yours is better! Drawing was never my forte!

Sigh.

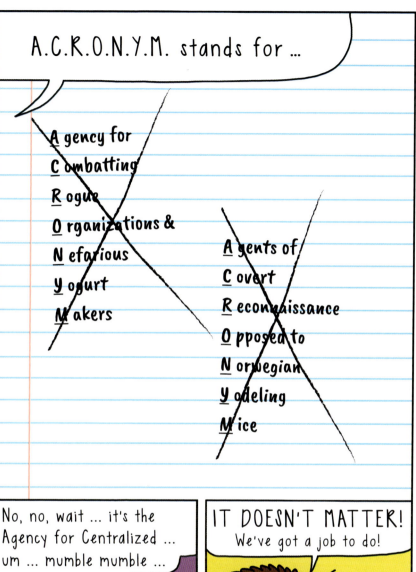

Chapter 9 **Super Dweeb Fan Club**

Some of Super Dweeb's (not lame) villains:

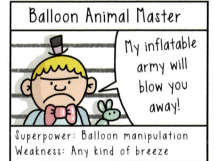

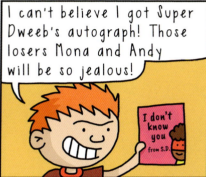

What a day! I was just about to go home and study when...

"SUPER DWEEB MERCHANDISE FOR SALE! Action figures! Foam replica pencils!"

NOOO! Oscar could blow everything! It wouldn't take much for someone to recognize him and realize that we're related! I stormed over.

"OSCAR!" I hissed!

STOMP!

"WHAT ON EARTH ARE YOU DOING?"

I said.

"Being your manager!" Oscar said.

"THE FANS WANT MERCHANDISE SO I MADE THIS ALL MYSELF!"

I tried not to get too angry.

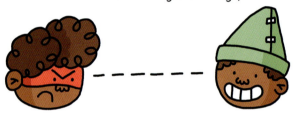

"COME IN HERE, QUICK!"

I said between clenched teeth and dragged Oscar into an alleyway.

Hey, my wagon!

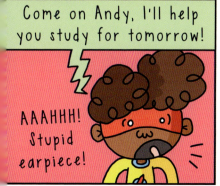

Chapter 10 Doctor Eraser-Butt's Secret Origin

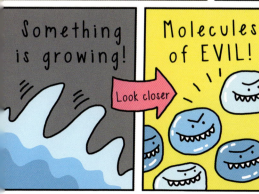

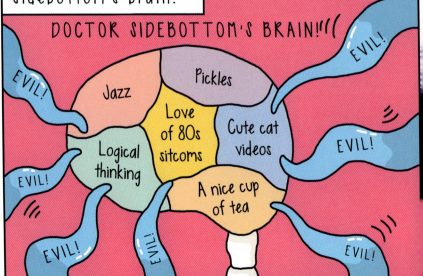

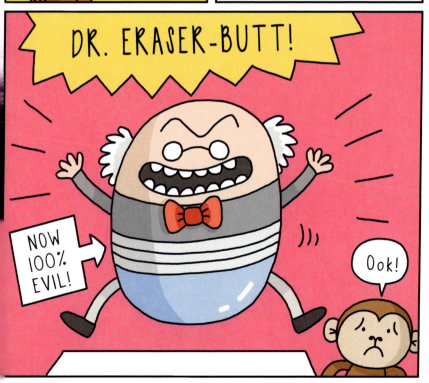

Chapter 11   No Ifs, One Butt

I was truly in the doghouse!

"I've got you a tutor," said Mom. "You can go to the library to study but then come straight home, no ifs or buts!"

"But I don't need a tutor!" I said. I stopped complaining when Mom threatened her death glare.

"Who's the tutor?" I asked.

"Mona is going to make sure you study instead of doodling your silly comic books," said Mom.

"I think you mean <u>EPIC</u> comic books!" I exclaimed.

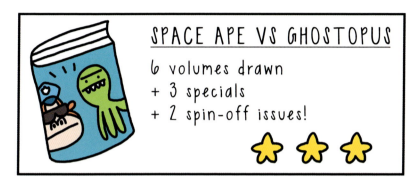

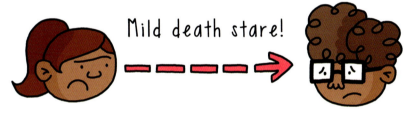

"Pass that test and you won't be grounded!"

Chapter 12   Kid Crayon Investigates

"Okay, we have a lead," said Mona. "I guess a villain who drops his business card can't be all that competent."

"So what now?" I asked.

"We hit the computer and find out what A.C.R.O.N.Y.M. means!" said Mona.

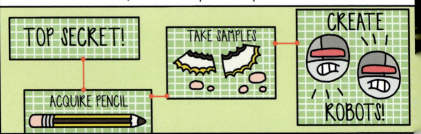

"The sample must have become contaminated somehow and made him EVIL!" Mona said.

"Not only is the science of this really confusing me, but the one time I get a decent villain, it turns out that I <u>created</u> him!" I wailed.

"Okay, so we break into A.C.R.O.N.Y.M.'s highly secured HQ, find the samples, **destroy** them, get out, and then <u>ACE</u> tomorrow's test!" Mona said.

"EASY PEASY," I said, queasily.

"Look, I can hack into the security cameras AND download a floor plan, so yeah! Easy!" said Mona.

I grumbled in resignation.

"Let's just get into the security feed and see what we're up against!" Mona tapped away on her computer. "OH NO!" she groaned.

"What is it?" I asked.

"It's Oscar! He's at A.C.R.O.N.Y.M. dressed as a ... crayon?

Okay, now all I had to do was sneak out of here before my parents noticed...

KNOCK KNOCK!

"Andy?" Mom called.

"Erk! Yes?" I squeaked.

"Dad and I are going to a P.T.A. MEETING so Amy is here to babysit. Is Oscar with you?"

"Um, yes! He's playing the quiet game!" I said.

Mona snorted through my earpiece. "SMOOTH!"

"When you've finished studying, put Oscar to bed, okay?"

"Sure, Mom. See you later!" I waited until I heard the front door close. "Phew! What a stroke of luck!"

"I can do better than that!" I said. "I'll draw a distraction that will distract the entire BUILDING!"

"GOOD IDEA," said Mona. "If we can cause enough chaos, no one will notice you sneaking around!"

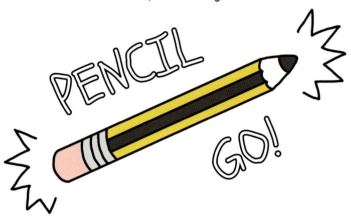

Chapter 13 Team-Up Time

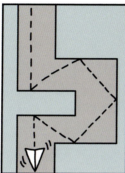
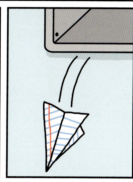

As I ran down the corridor trying to find Oscar, I saw a paper plane land on the floor.

"Hey, what's this?" I said.

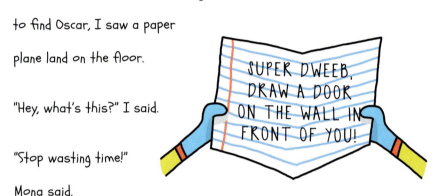

"Stop wasting time!" Mona said.

I opened the plane. "Oh, it's a letter!"

"Well, I can do that!" I said and drew a door on the wall with my pencil.

124

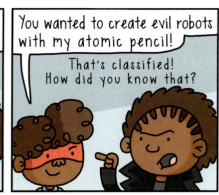
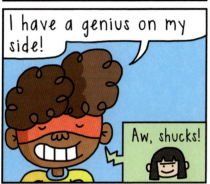

"I do," said Mona over my earpiece. "THE ONLY WAY TO STOP DR. ERASER-BUTT IS TO ERASE ..."

There was an awkward silence.

"Um, are you still there?" I asked.

Mona sighed. "That was a dramatic pause."

"Oh, sorry!" I said. "Carry on."

"You need to erase HIS BUTT."

I grinned. "Erase the eraser! We just need to get close enough to erase it!"

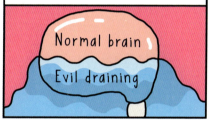

Chapter 14   Back at Dweeb HQ

"So thanks to all of you, the pencil samples have been destroyed and <u>WE'RE OVERHAULING ALL OF A.C.R.O.N.Y.M.</u>

"No more unstoppable cyborg armies!" said Agent Storm.

"PHEW!" I said.

"Maybe A.C.R.O.N.Y.M. could help us in the future," Mona said.

Agent Storm raised an eyebrow. "Maybe. And maybe we'll have some summer internships available too!"

I'm not sure the world is ready for Mona <u>AND</u> Agent Storm!

Agent Storm waved and left. "See you around!"

"Phew, what a day!" I said.

"Come on," said Mona. "We can squeeze in some last minute studying!"

I sighed. "Fine! We need to get home before Mom and Dad do. But I'll speak to you later?"

"You know it!" Mona said.

Andy's <u>new</u> report card

Test score: <u>**96/100**</u>

Mr. Squibb says: Andy's work has improved so much that I no longer think he is a pod person. <u>Well done!</u>

So everything pretty much worked out! <u>I ACED MY TEST</u>. Now I'm studying hard to get my grades back up and not letting my Andy-matter decoys do my homework! I've also learned that it can be **hard** to get the right balance between being a KID and a SUPERHERO.

FIN!

PART 3

SUPER DWEEB
VS
THE EVIL DOODLER

Chapter 15   Keeping Up with the Dweebs

"Andy!" Mr. Squibb shouted, for what I assumed wasn't the first time. Whoops, I was day-dreaming in class again!

You see, I've loved Gamma Guys comics ever since I was tiny and now they're ...

"Andy! The whole class is waiting to hear what you think about Romeo and Juliet!"

THE WHOLE CLASS ⟶ *We're really not...*

"Sorry Mr. Squibb, but the trailer for the GAMMA GUYS movie comes out tomorrow and I just can't concentrate!" I said.

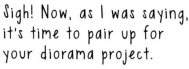

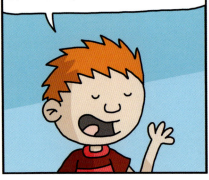

"Not all heroes wear capes, you know. Have you considered inspirational figures in your daily lives? A talented TEACHER, for example?"

But I wasn't really listening to Mr. Squibb. Someone called me their H E R O! How cool is that?

Even if it was Mean Mike who liked Super Dweeb, it still made me feel great.

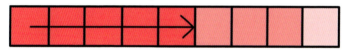

EGO METER

What are you grinning for? Just my luck to get paired with you!

I couldn't wait to tell Mona that I was a class project!

But it's still just school. Nowhere near as cool as ...

SECRET AGENT WORK EXPERIENCE!

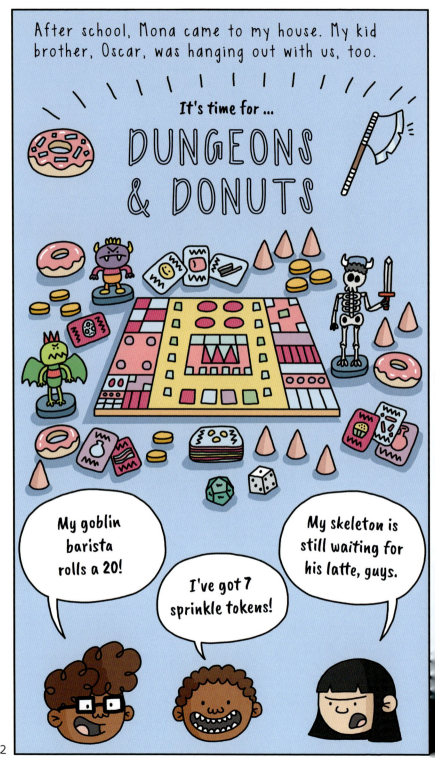

Chapter 16 Too Many Andys

"Speaking of <u>snacks</u>, looks like we've run out," I said. "Let me just draw something … !"

Scribble!

Draw!

POP!

"Doodle dupes, would you be so kind as to make me an ULTIMATE SANDWICH?"

Mona frowned. "I don't think making duplicates of yourself is such a great idea."

"But I can get so much more stuff done! They can do my chores, go and visit Grandma, and I can get on with more important things, like waiting for the GAMMA GUYS movie trailer to drop later today!"

"Speaking of a good thing, here comes my ultimate sandwich! My doodle dupes make it perfectly EVERY TIME!"

A closer look at the ultimate sandwich!

Bread
Ketchup
Pickles
Baloney
Popcorn
Mustard vein
Tortilla chips
Tomato
Marshmallows
Peanut butter
Bread

"I feel like that sandwich must be breaking some kind of law!" said Mona.

"It's so WRONG it must be RIGHT!" said Oscar.

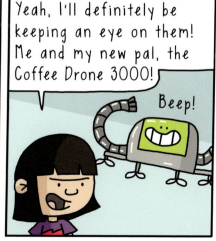

 "OOK! SNIFF! OOK!"

said Mr. Sniffles.

"Mr. Sniffles said that you shouldn't be stealing stuff from A.C.R.O.N.Y.M.," translated Oscar. "Their equipment is probably dangerous. Even the water coolers might have missiles!"

 "Okay, so firstly I'm just borrowing it so I can upgrade it! Also, it's a coffee drone! How dangerous could it be—"

 **DEATH MODE ENGAGED!**

 "**NO, DISENGAGE!** Heh, I need to tinker with it a bit!"

I quietly left Mona and Oscar to go and watch the Gamma Guys trailer, **FINALLY!**

"Mr. Sniffles says you're being a jerk!" said Oscar.

"Can you really understand what he's saying or are YOU just calling me a jerk?!"

"We have a special best-friend bond so I can understand him!"

"Fine, fine!" I grumbled. "Let me just go and get into my costume!"

"Gibble gibble!" said Mr. Sniffles.

(Translation: I have a bad feeling about this!)

And so ...

 DWEEB SQUAD READY!

Super Dweeb!

Kid Crayon

Mr. Sniffles and Tater-Tot!

"Okay," said Mona, "I've added a new Mona-Mode on the coffee drone so I can come with you in real-time but also stay here and use the computer!"

Mona!

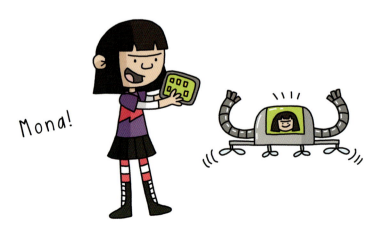

He draws his way out of trouble! SUPER DWEEB!

Do you need doodles on the double? SUPER DWEEB!

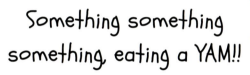

He can fix those villains with a biff and a WHAM!

Something something something, eating a YAM!!

Na na na na na na na naaaaaah...

He's the Super Dweeeeb!

Oscar says: I made this song up when I was in the bathtub!

153

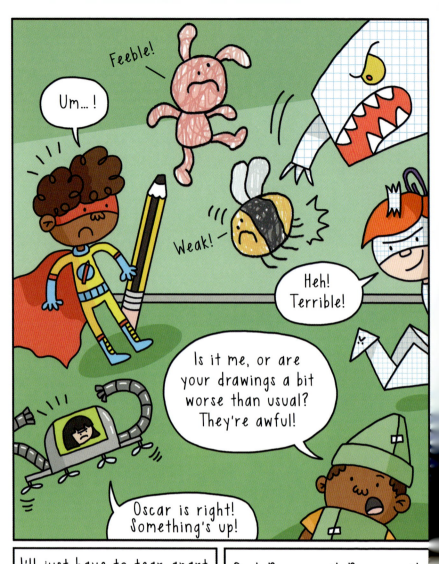

"That didn't go quite how I wanted it to," I grumbled.

The Mona-drone hovered near me. "While I'm VERY concerned that your pencil has a huge effect on paper, I'm more concerned about why it was malfunctioning."

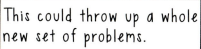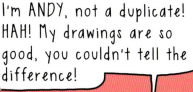

Chapter 17 Bad Times!

It's safe to say that everyone was REALLY mad at me.

"Well," said Mona through gritted teeth, "this is all basically awful but at least we've found out more about the pencil."

"I'm sure things aren't THAT bad," I said, weakly.

"Andy, you drew a duplicate pencil THAT ACTUALLY WORKED!" said Mona. "And your evil twin was REALLY angry!"

"But surely he'll just pop out of existence, like my other drawings?" I said.

"SCREECH! EEEK! OOK!" gibbered Mr. Sniffles.

"He said you'd better hope that Evil Andy doesn't come back here with an army," Oscar translated.

It's **SCIENCE TIME** with **MONA!**

Okay, this is what we know about the atomic pencil so far.

- It makes drawings come to life!
- Drawings last around 10 minutes when they come to life.
- Doodles can feed off graphite to last a bit longer.
- It's **VERY** bad when it falls into the wrong hands.

But the pencil can do other stuff too!

 Its eraser shavings have power.

Even paper with leftover doodles on it has radioactive power!

And the pencil can draw other pencils that work!

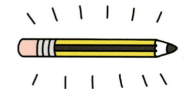

"So, now another version of Andy has an atomic pencil too!"

"He won't come back with an army!" I stuttered nervously.

"Let's just hope he doesn't find any graphite up in space before he pops out of existence," Mona said. "He was really angry at you, and I can't blame him!"

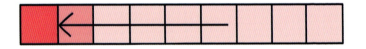

EGO METER

"And your pencil is getting blunt too!" said Oscar. "You're in trouble if he DOES come back for revenge!"

"He's going to come back with an army!!" I shrieked. "We have to prepare!!"

"I need to draw! I need to make my own army!"

Chapter 18   The Temple of Gloom

"Wait, Andy," Mona said. "I think I've worked out what's going on! The NEW pencil is draining power from the ORIGINAL one. That's why it won't work properly anymore."

"HOW DO WE FIX IT?!" I cried.

Mona pulled a piece of paper out of her pocket. "Remember this top-secret document I found at A.C.R.O.N.Y.M.? It looks like there's a <u>pencil sharpener</u> on this other island!"

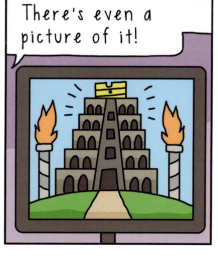

"It looks like whatever the sharpener is, it's in some kind of temple on this other island," said Mona.

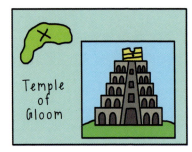

"How come you didn't know about this if you were handling <u>top-secret</u> documents?" I asked.

"I ... uh ... well ... gah! The truth is, I'm just a glorified photocopier! My internship is not as good as I thought it would be. I didn't want to tell you because I was embarrassed," Mona said.

"Mona, you're the smartest person I know and you're awesome! I don't care about how terrible your internship is. LOOK WHAT YOU FOUND!"

Mona grinned. "Thanks Andy! We'll talk about this more tomorrow. For now, we need a plan! I propose this: I'll take Mr. Sniffles and Tater-Tot and find this sharpener. You and Oscar get ready for the evil doodler and distract him until I get back!"

"Maybe if we feed Andy's wobbly drawings normal pencils they'll last longer!" said Oscar.

WE HAD A PLAN!

Dweeb Squad High Five!

Chapter 19 Andy Vs Anti-Andy

Back at Andy's house...

"Uh, I think your **EVIL TWIN** is coming!" said Oscar.

"These are all the normal pencils I can find. We'll feed them to my doodles and hope the graphite keeps them going!"

Come on, Andy! We can do this! No evil clone can defeat us! Especially if he's as dumb as you are!

"RUDE!" I said. "But I get your point, Oscar— **LET'S DO THIS!**"

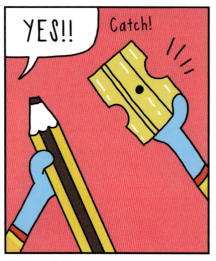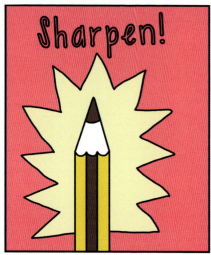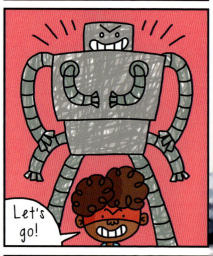

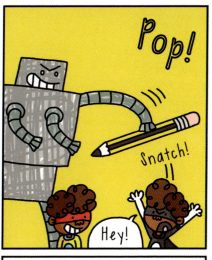

"Well," said Mona, "While I'm sure all of that could have been avoided, things worked out!"

"I've learned a valuable lesson, too!" I said.

"Not to take your doodles for granted?" asked Oscar.

"Uh, that too! But also that we should probably leave before we get blamed for the huge meteor over there! Let's go!"

"Yeep!" said Mr. Sniffles.

Back at Mona's, we were ready to get back into our game of Dungeons and Donuts...

"I think we need to keep an eye on A.C.R.O.N.Y.M.! They've found Fallout Island and they're up to something!"

"Are you going to quit your internship, Mona?" I asked.

"No," said Mona. "I'm going to work from the inside! I'll keep photocopying and pretend not to know anything! They'll never suspect me."

"Like a real spy! Awesome!"

"Even better— a spy who spies on spies."

"You know, we have a pretty good team here!

We've got a Super Dweeb ..."

"A secret agent!"   "A sidekick!"   "A monkey!"   "And a dog!"

"And I will go and get us some awesome snacks all by myself, with no help from my doodles!" I said.

"Just *one thing*, Andy," said Mona.

"Please don't make us an **ULTIMATE SANDWICH,** though. It just looks gross."

"I actually really liked it!" said Oscar.

How to draw ANDY

Follow these simple steps to draw your own Super Dweeb!

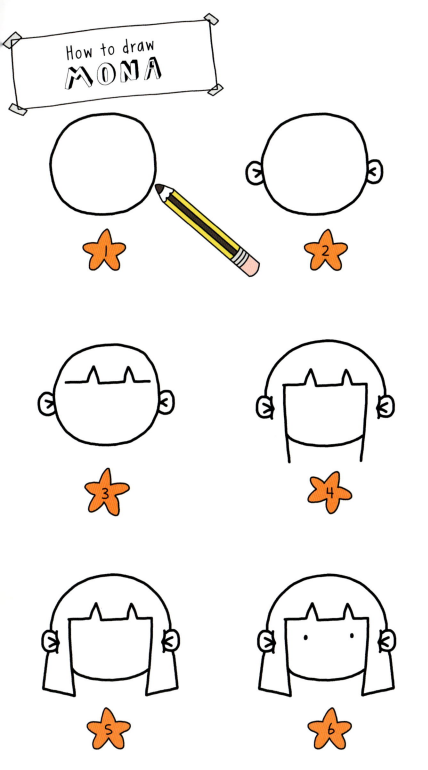

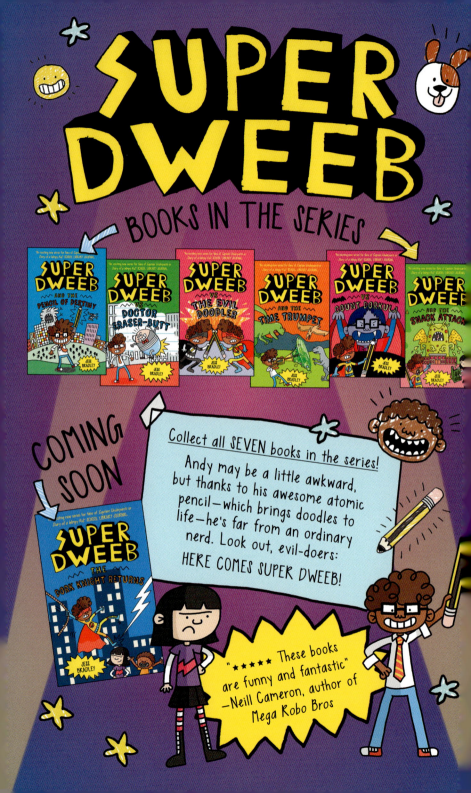

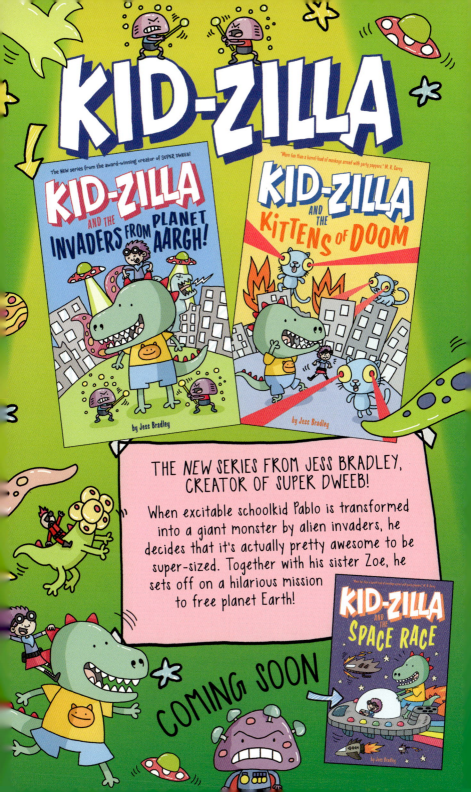

ABOUT THE AUTHOR

Jess Bradley is an illustrator and comic artist who lives in Devon, England. She's drawn quite a few books over the years and loves to work on all-ages comics. She writes and illustrates a regular strip called "Squid Bits" for The Phoenix magazine. In 2021, a book illustrated by Jess (A Day In The Life Of A Poo, A Gnu and You) won the Blue Peter Award for Best Non-Fiction.

Jess enjoys doodling in her sketchbooks, watching scary movies, reading, and playing video games. She once jumped out of a plane (with a parachute).

Thanks for reading!